A Book of Friendship
Celebrating the Joys of Having Friends

Edited by Kitty McDonald Clevenger
Illustrated with a colorful collection of photography,
stitchery, cartoons and contemporary art

Hallmark Crown Editions

Acknowledgments: "That's What Friends Are For." Words and music
by Paul Williams. © 1972 Almo Music Corp. (ASCAP). All Rights
Reserved. Int'l. Copyright Secured. Used by permission. "To My Friend" from
Some Brighter Dawn by Grace Noll Crowell. Copyright 1943 by Harper & Row,
Publishers, Inc. By permission of the publisher. "On Friendship" reprinted
from *The Prophet* by Kahlil Gibran, with permission of the publisher,
Alfred A. Knopf, Inc. Copyright 1923 by Kahlil Gibran; renewal copyright
1951 by Administrators C.T.A. of Kahlil Gibran Estate, and Mary G.
Gibran. "Harry Is Alive" from *Pageant of Adventure* by Lowell Thomas.
Reprinted with permission of the author. "Me" from *Bells and Grass* by
Walter de la Mare. Copyright 1941 by Walter de la Mare. Copyright ©
renewed 1969 by Richard de la Mare. Reprinted by permission of The
Viking Press, The Literary Trustees of Walter de la Mare, and The Society
of Authors as their representative. "Miscellaneous File" by Dorothy Brown
Thompson from *The Kansas City Star,* 1939. Reprinted with permission of
the author.

That's What Friends Are For

Friends are like music —
Sometimes they're sad.
Sometimes they're lonely
and need to be told
that they're loved.
Everyone needs to be loved.

Friends are like good wine
And I've had the best.
Don't always show it
But no one knows better than I.

Friends are like warm clothes
In the night air —
Best when they're old.
And we miss them the most when they're gone.
Miss them the most when they're gone.

Friends love your good side
And live with your bad.
Want you and need you
When no one else knows you're alive.

Paul Williams

A Friend

A Friend is one who incessantly pays us the compliment of expecting from us all the virtues, and who can appreciate them in us.

The Friend asks no return but that his Friend will religiously accept and wear and not disgrace his apotheosis of him. They cherish each other's hopes. They are kind to each other's dreams.

That kindness which has so good a reputation elsewhere can least of all consist with this relation, and no such affront can be offered to a Friend, as a conscious good-will, a friendliness which is not a necessity of the Friend's nature.

Friendship is never established as an understood relation. It is a miracle which requires constant proofs. It is an exercise of the purest imagination and of the rarest faith.

We do not wish for Friends to feed and clothe our bodies — neighbors are kind enough for that — but to do the life office to our spirit. For this, few are rich enough, however well disposed they may be....

The language of Friendship is not words, but meanings. It is an intelligence above language.

Henry David Thoreau

This Old Street

This old street
Is my old street,
I would not change it for the world,
I've seen it dressed
In April's best,
When all its petals were unfurled.

I've seen it asleep
And buried deep
Beneath a shroud of ermine snow,
And in the fall,
When wild geese call,
Leaves tumble to the ground below.

I've seen it lie
In the heat of July
Waiting for Summer's cooling rain,
As through the days,
I've walked these ways,
Sometimes in joy, sometimes in pain.

At every stage,
I've watched it age
In pleasant and inclement weather,
And around each bend
I've met a friend,
For we have grown old together.

Mary Ellen Stelling

Hello

I took the time to say "hello"
To someone that I didn't know,
To someone who was walking by —
A look of sadness in her eyes.

And when she smiled back gratefully
And said a warm "hello" to me,
I realized my "little gift"
Had given both of us a lift!

You never know just whom you'll meet
Throughout your day on any street —
People just like me and you
With loneliness and problems, too.

Yet life is always better when
We take the time to be a friend
To someone we don't even know —
And all it takes is one "hello."

Richie Tankersley

Charles M. Schulz

Definition

Limping I dragged my weary well-scarred body
to my friend.
"Fool!" she shrilled. "I told you that you couldn't fly!
Oh fool!"
She was truly wise and I recognized her wisdom.
Why then did I limp on,
to my friend across the way —
My friend who saw me come in tears
and said,
"It didn't work this time?
Let's see, perhaps we still can mend this wing —
a feather here and there —
Rest: we'll see what we can do."

Jan Churchill

A True Friend

What is friendship? Alas, I am able to give you an
example. A number of years ago a very intimate friend
of my college days, whom everyone had regarded as a
perfect example of integrity, was accused in the
newspapers of a crime. I could not believe it. I was so
certain of his virtue that I wrote him a letter in which
I said that I and all his friends were certain that he had
not done anything wrong, that he had been slandered,
and that he must not feel too bad about the attack,
because as long as he had the inner certainty that he
had done nothing wrong, he could remain calm and
serene. I received a very affectionate letter in return,
and then a few days later he committed suicide. Of
course, I can't be certain whether I was in any way
responsible for this tragedy; but what I am certain of
is that I wrote him a very bad letter and that I was
untrue in friendship.

Some years after this I was the subject of an attack
because a press dispatch quoted me as having said
something I really had not said. I received a letter from
one of my former pupils. This is what he wrote to me:

"I do not believe that the report of your remarks is
true. I do not see how you could have said that; but I
want you to know that even if you did say it, my
friendship and affection for you will always remain the
same."

That is a good letter. That is friendship.

William Lyon Phelps

Norman LaLiberte

Harv Gariety

Celebrate

Make every day a holiday...
celebrate the sky,
celebrate the trees and grass,
the bees and butterflies.
Celebrate the birds that sing
and flowers that smell so sweet,
the sun up high above your head,
the earth beneath your feet.
And celebrate the smiles you see,
the cheerful words you hear,
celebrate each moment
that you spend with loved ones near.
Celebrate the happiness
that friends are always giving...
make every day a holiday,
and celebrate...just living!

Karen Ravn

"Harry Is Alive"

At Las Vegas, New Mexico, Carl Myers spoke up and said: "The Carnegie Medal? What do I care about the medal? Harry is alive, isn't he?" Yes, Harry Reid was alive, and that was reward enough for Carl Myers.

They were both miners, and they planted eleven charges of dynamite in an eighty-five-foot shaft. They cut the fuses long enough so they'd be able to climb up to a higher level, where they'd be safe from the blast. Then they lighted the fuses and ran. Carl scampered up the incline. But before Harry could make it, one charge of dynamite went off prematurely, and hurled him down, unconscious, hundreds of splinters piercing his legs. Carl yelled to him. No response. And there were those other ten charges of dynamite, fuses lighted and sputtering! If they exploded with Harry down there, that would be the end of Harry.

Carl took a jump down the incline. The fuses were burning short, the dynamite might go any minute. Carl picked up his unconscious pal, flung him across his shoulder, and started up the steep twenty-five-foot slope. It was a muscle-breaking job — he had to go mighty fast. Just as he got to the top to safety, dumped Harry down and fell exhausted — the dynamite roared.

The mine owners announced that they were going to recommend Carl Myers for the Carnegie Award for Heroism. But Carl just growled: — "Damn the medal, Harry is alive, isn't he?"

Lowell Thomas

Tom Di Grazia

To My Friend

Because you are my friend
I long today
To bring you some imperishable gift
Of beauty.
Something glowing and warm
Like the coals of living fire,
Something as cool and sweet
As lilies at dawn,
Something as restful and clean
As smooth white sheets at night
When one is very tired,
Something with the taste of spring water
From high places,
Or like the tang of cool purple grapes
To the mouth.
But O my friend,
Since I cannot buy such gifts for you,
Come go with me
Out into the little everyday fields of living,
And let us gather in our baskets, like manna,
God's gift to us:
The down-pouring, exquisite beauty
Of life itself.

Grace Noll Crowell

Wanted, a Friend!

We hear of people seeking, by public advertisement, a suitable partner in marriage, but who ever heard of any one's advertising for a friend? Yet why not? Every one, it is likely, has in mind some more or less vague ideal of the absolutely perfect comrade. May he not be supposed to exist somewhere, and to be in the habit of reading a daily newspaper or a monthly magazine? Go to! Let us seek him, then, by appropriate advertisement. Something in this wise would it run?

"Wanted, a Friend!... The applicant must be rather old, in order to be fitted to give advice — a limited amount of it — wisely; and at the same time rather young, in order to receive it in liberal quantity and in a meek frame of mind. He must be of medium height, intellectually, and in the enjoyment of robust spiritual health. A written guarantee must be given of freedom from all contagious defects of character!"

Edward Rowland Sill

Friends

Friends are made
Of bread and cheese
And applesauce and honey
And odds and ends that,
Quick as a wink,
Make eyes and hearts so sunny.

Living joyously and well,
Content with
What comes after,
Friends are made
Of fine-combed love
With golden threads of laughter.

Sarah Bridge Graves

There is no scale or chart on earth
To measure what a friend is worth.

Ralph Waldo Emerson

Little friends may prove
great friends.

Aesop

John Trotta

Friendship is . . .

Friendship is Congeniality
  a fitting together
    like the pieces
      of a
    jigsaw puzzle

a mix-'n'-matching
    of moods and tastes
  of interests and abilities . . .
of needs and plenty.

Friendship is a Bridge
Across it pass
  those things
    we long to share . . .
  our hopes . . .
    our dreams . . .
  our heartaches . . .
    our triumphs . . .
  and
    our failures.

Friendship is a Treasure Chest
of memories . . .
  and thoughts of things
    friends have done
    to make life
      richer . . .
        brighter . . .
          more beautiful . . .

Friends
  are treasures —
    more precious than
    gold or jewels.

Friendship is a Rainbow
spanning the distance
    between friends...
with all its colors meaningful —
    its red...love...
    its orange...warmth...
    its yellow...joy...
    its green...hope...
    its blue...loyalty...
    its violet...suffering....
Friends share them all.

Friendship is Magnetic
an attraction...
    an affinity...

    a resemblance...
        a connection...

an intimacy...
    drawing us
        to another person.

True Friends are Rare
They must
    penetrate
        the forest
of our
    littleness
        and faults...

and discover
    our potential greatness
        and our efforts
            to attain it.

Sister Constance Mary

27

Loretta Schuster

My Friend

I love you not only for what you are,
but for what I am when I am with you.

I love you not only for what you have made
of yourself, but for what you are making of me.

I love you because you have done more than any creed
could have done to make me good, and more
than any fate could have done to make me happy.

You have done it without a touch,
without a word, without a sign.

You have done it by being yourself. Perhaps
that is what being a friend means, after all.

Roy Croft

AMEN!

Miscellaneous File

Just why should friends be chronological,
Fraternal friends, or pedagogical,
Alike in race or taste or color —
It only makes the meetings duller!
Unclassified by tribe or steeple,
Why shouldn't friends be merely people?

Dorothy Brown Thompson

Androcles and the Lion

Once there was a young man named Androcles. He was a slave to a Winemaker, who was also a drunkard. And when the Winemaker drank wine he often beat Androcles. After suffering many beatings, Androcles decided to run away.

He was several miles from the vineyard when all of a sudden he came upon a Lion. He was about to run away when he noticed the Lion was hurt. He crept up to the animal and found that he had a huge thorn in his paw. With utmost care Androcles removed the thorn. The Lion was so grateful that he led Androcles to his den, fed him what he had to offer, and made him lie down for a nap. They became such good friends that Androcles decided to stay awhile. Every day the Lion went hunting for food for Androcles. It was proving to be a nice arrangement when one day the two of them were captured by hunters.

As Androcles later learned, the hunters had been sent by his old master. To get his revenge, the master decided to starve the Lion for several days and then turn him loose on Androcles. When the time came, the two were thrown into a large arena. The Lion ran toward Androcles, his lips curled back and his long teeth sparkling. But when he reached Androcles he jumped on him and licked him lovingly on the cheek.

The master was so impressed by this show of affection that Androcles and the Lion were given their freedom, a nourishing meal, and all the wine they could carry.

Aesop

On Friendship

And a youth said, Speak to us of Friendship.
And he answered, saying:
Your friend is your needs answered.
He is your field which you sow with love
    and reap with thanksgiving.
And he is your board and your fireside.
For you come to him with your hunger,
    and you seek him for peace....

When you part from your friend, you grieve not;
For that which you love most in him
    may be clearer in his absence,
    as the mountain to the climber
    is clearer from the plain.
And let there be no purpose in friendship
    save the deepening of the spirit.
For love that seeks aught but the disclosure
    of its own mystery is not love
    but a net cast forth:
    and only the unprofitable is caught.

And let your best be for your friend.
If he must know the ebb of your tide,
    let him know its flood also.
For what is your friend that you should seek him
    with hours to kill?

Seek him always with hours to live.
For it is his to fill your need,
   but not your emptiness.
And in the sweetness of friendship
   let there be laughter,
   and sharing of pleasures.
For in the dew of simple things
   the heart finds its morning
   and is refreshed.

Kahlil Gibran from The Prophet

Charles Schorre

What Men Live By

Russian author Leo Tolstoy once wrote a brief allegory in which an Angel disguised as a man is sent to earth by God to learn these three lessons: what is given to men, what is not given to men, and what men live by. At the conclusion of the story, the Angel reveals his identity to the poor shoemaker who had taken him in, and speaks of the lessons he has learned.

The clothes fell off the body of the Angel, and he was clothed with light so that no eye could bear to look upon him, and he began to speak more terribly, as if his voice did not come from him, but from Heaven. And the Angel said:

"I learnt that man does not live by care for himself, but by love for others. It was not given the mother to know what was needful for the life of her children; it was not given to the rich man to know what was needful for himself; and it is not given to any man to know whether by the evening he will want boots for his living body or slippers for his corpse. When I came to earth as a man, I lived not by care for myself, but by the love that was in the heart of a passerby, and his wife, and because they were kind and merciful to me.

The orphans lived not by any care they had for themselves; they lived through the love that was in the heart of a stranger, a woman who was kind and merciful to them. *And all men live, not by reason of any care they have for themselves, but by the love for them that is in other people.*

"I knew before that God gives life to men, and desires them to live; but now I know far more. I know that God does not desire men to live apart from each other, and therefore has not revealed to them what is needful for each of them to live by himself. He wishes them to live together united, and therefore has revealed to them that they are needful to each other's happiness."

Walter Chandoha

Me

As long as I live
I shall always be
My Self — and no other,
Just me.

Like a tree —

Willow, elder,
Aspen, thorn,
Or cypress forlorn.

Like a flower,
For its hour —
Primrose, or pink,
Or a violet —
Sunned by the sun,
And with dewdrops wet.

Always just me.

Walter de la Mare

Good Ol' Cherry Pie

From east to west,
from north to south,
there's nothing better
for your mouth
than good ol' cherry pie!
You can eat it
hot or cold,
when you're young
and when you're old.
Eat it morning,
night or noon
with your fingers,
fork or spoon.
Eat it plain
or a la mode,
in your abode
or on the road!
Just grab a slice
and go to town,
use some milk
to wash it down.
Once you start
it's hard to stop,
you'll want to eat it
till you pop!

If you don't like it
you really must
be flakier
than any crust,
'cause any time
or any place
with anything,
in any case,
the greatest thing
to feed your face
is good ol' cherry pie!

Karen Ravn

The Truest Friend

A dog is a comfort,
    an ally in a sometimes unfriendly world.
A dog is a welcoming committee
    that lets you know you're home, all right!
A dog is the certainty that home is where you most
    want to be.
A dog is a chance to express yourself
    without the fear of seeming foolish,
a chance to share emotions that others of our kind
    too often repel — tenderness, outright joy, love.
A dog hears your secret needs and sympathizes
    or artfully distracts you from your woes.
A dog defeats loneliness, defies unhappiness
    and teaches hard humans the virtue of play.
A dog gives you the feeling, however untrue,
    that you're worth his affection.
A dog holds to values this world has forgotten —
    duty, loyalty, respect.
A dog will obey you, bestowing upon a master
    power one's own children come to challenge.
Most of all, especially in times like these,
    a dog is the truest and most reliable friend.

Gail Peterson

Ode to a Cat

There is nothing quite so restful as a cat
When the weary day is ended
And your head is bowed and bended
Who is nicer to come home to than a cat?
Just like the peaceful waves upon a distant shore
Never yammering or yowling
Just a courteous meowing
When the little beastie greets you at the door.
Although a dog may be appealing
Firm and faithful in his dealing
All his love for you revealing
This won't change the way I feel
I'm standing pat, I like a cat
He is always welcome to my welcome mat.
No, there is nothing so relaxing as a cat
It's a pleasure to observe him
Nothing ever can unnerve him
With a cat you know exactly where you're at
No, there's nothing quite so restful as a cat.

Herbert B. Greenhouse

Saul Steinberg

A Friend's Greeting

I'd like to be the sort of friend
    that you have been to me;
I'd like to be the help that you've been
    always glad to be;
I'd like to mean as much to you
    each minute of the day
As you have meant, old friend of mine,
    to me along the way.

I'd like to do the big things
    and the splendid things for you,
To brush the gray from out your skies
    and leave them only blue;
I'd like to say the kindly things
    that I so oft have heard,
And feel that I could rouse your soul
    the way that mine you've stirred.

I'd like to give you back the joy
    that you have given me,
Yet that were wishing you a need
    I hope will never be;
I'd like to make you feel as rich as I,
    who travel on
Undaunted in the darkest hours
    with you to lean upon.

I'm wishing as the days go on
    that I could but repay
A portion of the gladness
    that you've strewn along my way;
And could I have one wish this year,
    this only would it be:
I'd like to be the sort of friend
    that you have been to me.

Edgar A. Guest

Fred Klemushin

The Friend in Your Mirror

Speak gently to yourself.
  Speak freely
in praise of all you are.
  Speak clearly
with pride in all you've been.
  Speak bravely
with hope for all you may become.
  Find in yourself
the powers that only you possess,
  the pains
that only you can overcome,
  the promises
that only you can keep.
  Look deeply
into the mirror of your life
    and discover the very special person
        that only you can be.

Edward Cunningham

How true!

Set in Bembo, a Venetian face first cut in 1495
by Francesco Griffo for the printer
Aldus Manutius Romanus and named by the latter
in honor of the humanist poet Pietro Bembo.
Printed on Hallmark Eggshell Book paper.
Designed by William M. Gilmore.